Ten
Walks Around
COVENTRY

by Coventry Ramblers Association
edited by John Roberts with
sketches by Norman Finnerty

W*ALKWAYS

****

WALKWAYS
J S Roberts
8 Hillside Close, Bartley Green
Birmingham B32 4LT

****

Ten Walks
around Coventry

by Coventry Ramblers Association
edited by John Roberts
with sketches by Norman Finnerty.

ISBN 0 947708 32 4

First Published 1995

Publisher's Note & Standing Offer

After seeing *Twenty Walks around Rugby* which I published for Rugby Ramblers, the Coventry Group of the Ramblers Association asked if I would like to publish a book of walks for them.

When we met to discuss the project I was able to offer a range of services. The Group could just hand me what they had written and I would arrange for printing, or I could edit their work, or I could do further research and supplement it, or I could walk the paths and rewrite the directions, etc etc.

In the event they sent me their walk descriptions and decided that I should follow all the paths and provide a new text. I was able to do this and extend the comment and information, supply sketches and present them with a full draft of an expanded manuscript written from a fresh viewpoint. My usual WALKWAYS format and approach suited the Group, though they could have had any other they wished. At all times the Group had the final say on the wording, but actually changed very little of what I wrote. It was highly enjoyable.

Here then, is a standing offer to any RA Group in England or Wales who want to publish their own book of local walks. I will provide any level of service you choose, from simply arranging the printing through to walking your paths and (if you wish) writing your book from scratch. The financial arrangements are attractive and not affected by how much work I do.

John Roberts
WALKWAYS

WALKWAYS

DaywalkS Footpath Networks

Networks of linked paths cover each area.

Cannock Chase (£4.20)
Vale of Llangollen (£4.20)
Wyre Forest (£4.20)

Strolls & Walks

From twenty places there is a short stroll and a walk.

Strolls & Walks from Picnic Places (Midlands) (£3.95)
Strolls & Walks from Cotswold Villages (£5.50)
Strolls & Walks from Midland Villages (1996)

Long Distance Routes

Step by step guides in both directions

Centenary Way (1996) Birmingham to Aberystwyth (1996)
Llangollen to Snowdon (1997) Birmingham to Bala (some time)
Heart of England Way (£5.50)

Walks around :::

Walks in specific areas by Ramblers Association groups.

Twenty Walks around Rugby (£3.75)
Twenty Walks around Stourbridge (1996)

**8 Hillside Close, Bartley Green, Birmingham
B32 4LT   021 550 3158
(write or phone for catalogue)**

Meet Coventry
Ramblers Association

Coventry Group of the Ramblers Association was formed in 1983. It has grown into a friendly and dynamic group of people which is going from strength to strength.

We organise about 100 walks a year. Most start at 10.00 am on Sundays and they vary between 5 and 10 miles. We explore our local area - Warwickshire, Staffordshire, Oxfordshire, Northants and Worcestershire, and sometimes go further with coach trips and holidays to the Peak District, the Cotswolds, Wenlock Edge and Wales. Our social events include bowls, barbecues, beer and skittles and barn dances.

A primary aim of the Ramblers Association is to protect our public footpaths, bridleways and green lanes and there are some 400 in our Group's territory. We have friendly relations with local farmers and report broken down stiles, blockages and the need for waymarking to Warwickshire County or Coventry City Council. We also comment on diversion proposals or other developments which might affect paths, sometimes agreeing, sometimes objecting.

Walking is Britain's most popular recreation. This is recognised by the Countryside Commission who have set local Councils the target of having all paths in their areas clearly marked and unobstructed by the year 2000. We are doing our best to help the local bodies meet it.

In 1995 the Ramblers Association celebrated its Jubilee Year - 60 years of working for walkers. This book is the Coventry Groups contribution. By sharing and enjoying these local walks you will be celebrating with us and helping the Countryside Commission to hit the target. They can all be reached by bus or car, they are easy, pleasant and interesting and will give you a real taste of the walking we can offer.

Many thanks to all members of the group who helped in any way with this book, by contributing walks, writing or testing them or by distributing it. Thanks in particular to John Roberts without whose help it would not have been possible.

We hope that you will enjoy these walks, and if you would like more in good company, Coventry Ramblers Association will give you a warm welcome. You can get contact names and phone numbers from Libraries or Tourist Information Centres which also have copies of our programme, you can reach us through RA's National Office at 1/5 Wandsworth Road London, SW8 2XX (0171 582 6878), or by phoning me on 01203 402953.

Janet Satchwell
Chairman
October 1995

Dedication

This book is dedicated to Alec May,
keen walker and good friend, and commemorates
the 60th Jubilee Year of the Ramblers Association.

step alive!

1935/1995

Contents

Coventry & its Landscapes   (1)

Boots and Clothes and Things   (3)

Rights of Way & Obstructions   (3)

Amendment Service   (4)

Using the Directions   (4)

Getting to the Start   (6)

List of Walks   (6)

General Map   (7)

Coventry & its Landscapes

The sixty miles of walking in this book leads you by ancient
trackways, deep lanes, quiet field paths, secret ponds, old
churches and slumbering villages - and all on Coventry's
doorstep. At the Heart of England you can see the Gospel
Oak where John Wesley preached, see yourself reflected in
a holy well, and may find that Tipperary is nearer than you
thought. Each walk has descriptions of its main features but
here we can sketch some of the themes.

Coventry lies in a saucer shaped bowl surrounded by higher
ground and three different types of landscape. To the north-
east, roughly the sector between Bedworth and Brinklow,
is the High Cross Plateau, which you meet on the Ansty
and Barnacle walk. Here you pass through the remnants of
Coventry's first green belt and the Warwickshire coalfield
to the cold, enclosed fields which ripple away towards
Leicestershire.

To the south-east and south of the City is the low, wet,
gravelly valley of the River Avon before the ground rises
towards Dunsmore Heath. Odd patches of roadside gorse
here are the legacy of the old heathland plants. Across
Coventry's north-west edge lies the Corley - Atherstone
ridge, a sandstone outcrop which peters out west side of
the City.

Finally and perhaps best of all, is the Arden country to the
west. It has several different faces and experts divide it
in this way. *Ancient Arden* is an intimate landscape of farms
on small hills with irregular fields and narrow, winding
lanes. You will meet it to the north and north-west, an area
of former wood pastures and heath with patches of ancient
woodland, mature hedgerow oaks and scattered half timbered
and brick settlements. *Industrial Arden* is a mixed and often

run down urban fringe, with old mining settlements, spoil heaps and pockets of bleak farmland. *Arden Parklands* has gently rolling landscapes between belts of trees and patches of woodland. *Wooded Estatelands* have larger rolling hills and valley with prominent hilltop woodlands. Finally, *Arden River Valleys* are narrow, meandering corridors with waterside trees and grazing meadows.

You will meet all of these features on our walks and often several in a short stretch. Between Burton Green and Balsall Common you pass from estate and parkland to pastures which survived the end of common land in the 17th and 18th century inclosures. Around Temple Balsall, Barston and Fen End is the wandering valley of the River Blythe with its wetland grazing.

The River Blythe flows into the River Tame which joins the Trent, and eventually runs into the North Sea. So does the River Anker from the Nuneaton area. But Coventry's own rivers, the Sherbourne and Sowe, and all the rivers south and west of the city, flow into the Avon to join the River Severn and escape to the Bristol Channel. The line of higher ground which separates these two great river basins is the main watershed of England, and you cross it near Meriden, Corley and Kinwalsey.

So Warwickshire is not flat and featureless, and at points on these walks you will see most of our Midland hills and uplands - the Cotswolds, Lickeys, Clent, the Wrekin, the Malverns, Arbury Hill, Charnwood Forest, the Peak District and Cannock Chase. Coventry's local volcano was at Oldbury, near Nuneaton but is fortunately extinct. Enjoy the panorama, but look back at Coventry in the middle of all this wonderful countryside.

Walking is man's natural pace in the countryside, you can see and hear so much more, smell the air and feel the breeze. Coventry RA Group wish you good walking and many happy memories.

Boots and Clothes and Things

These walks are all modest affairs and you do not need to go equipped for mountaineering. There are many books that offer sound advice on boots, clothing and equipment if you want to take up walking as a pastime.

This part of the Midlands can be very muddy in wet weather. Walking boots are best, but for short walks wellies will do fine if you find them comfortable. Trainers are excellent in dry weather. You do not necessarily need two pairs of socks but a good thickness of woolly padding is a great comfort. The traditional grey, rough wool ragsock is hardwearing and reasonably thick, but that is about all. Try loop pile socks. It will usually be sensible to take a hat and waterproof.

Rights of Way & Obstructions

These walks are all on public Rights of Way or in places where the public is permitted to walk. They may be Footpaths, Bridleways or Byways (usually green lanes or tracks) with some stretches of ordinary road. Your rights as pedestrian are the same on all, you are entitled to follow the track or cross the land. The fact that it is "private" (most land is) is quite irrelevant.

Occupiers of land are legally obliged not to obstruct paths, it is an offence, but sometimes they do. Paths should not be ploughed up nor have crops growing over them, nor should you meet barbed wire fences. You are entitled to cross or remove any such obstacles doing as little damage as you reasonably can. You may diverge to pass the obstacle so long as you go no further than necessary and do not enter someone else's land.

These notes appear in all WALKWAYS books but you are unlikely to meet real problems on these walks. If you do, please contact us or phone messages through the publisher.

Amendment Service

The countryside changes all the time. You could meet new tracks, stiles and barns; hedges vanish and paths may be diverted. To keep directions as up to date as possible WALKWAYS issues amendment slips.

IF you write to tell of any changes or problems that you meet, stating route and paragraph number, they will refund your postage.

IF you send a stamped addressed envelope with a note of what books you have, they will send you up to date amendment slips. (Telephone enquiries welcome - 0121 550 3158)

Using the Directions

You will see that the Directions are quite separate from the description and comment, very terse and set in short, narrow, numbered paragraphs in a clear and open typeface. These and less obvious features have been adopted for WALKWAYS books after much experience and thought. The aim is to give you information in easily located and remembered blocks of convenient a size, bearing in mind that you will be reading them on the move.

Distances in YARDS or MILES are to give a rough idea how far to walk. You do not have to try and measure because you will be given something to look out for. Distance in PACES are there to be counted out, if you need to. Paces vary but you can allow for being very tall or short. The reason for all this is that people carry a pace with them but not usually a measuring tape, and very few of us have got a clue what 200 yards looks like.

The maps are sketches to an approximate scale of 2.5ins/ 1mile. They are more to confirm where you are rather than for route finding. The meanings of the symbols are mainly obvious but we show a few of them below. The numbers of selected paragraphs from the route descriptions appear on the maps. The big black arrow on each map points north.

Start of Walk	●	Path	....
Track	- - - ._	Road	━━━
Fence/Hedge	⌐	Woodland	ᵕᵕᵕ

For each walk we note the relevant Ordnance Survey maps. In fact, you should manage the walks very well with the directions and sketch maps, but a general map of the area is necessary to find starting points. A good road atlas will do. The well known *A to Z* of Birmingham & West Midlands is a street map. However it covers most of these walks, or at least, the starting points, so we have given references.

The Ordnance Survey Landranger series (1.25 inches/mile; 2 cms/km) are the most convenient to carry for general interest. You would need sheets 139 Birmingham, and 140 Leicester & Coventry.

The more detailed Pathfinder sheets (2.5 inches/mile; 4 cms/ km) are for people really addicted to maps. They will need sheets, 935 (SP28/38) Coventry North & Meriden, and 955 (SP27/37) Coventry South and Kenilworth.

Getting to the Start

These walks have been carefully chosen so that you can reach starting points by bus or car.

BUSES
Bus services and their numbers may well change. The best we can do is tell you in each case where to find the bus stop. To find the service number and current times phone the Centro Hotline on 0121 200 2700 or 01203 559559. They can send you bus maps of Coventry and Solihull showing all the services.

CARS
We have made sure that there are suitable places for a few cars near starting points. Please use a car park if there is one and take great care never to cause any obstruction or inconvenience. If the bus stop or best parking place is a short way from the starting point we give directions to it.

List of Walks

	miles/kms	Pge
Ansty & Barnacle	5.5/9	(9)
Barston & Wootton Green	6.5/11	(13)
Brandon, Brinklow & Bretford	5.5/9	(19)
Burton Green & Balsall Common	5/9.5	(21)
Burton Green & Crackley Wood	5.5/9	(25)
Eastern Green & Meriden	5/8	(28)
Keresley & Corley	5/8	(32)
Meriden & Kinwalsey	5.5/9	(37)
Temple Balsall & Fen End	5.5/9	(41)
Wall Hill & Harvest Hill	5.5/9	(45)

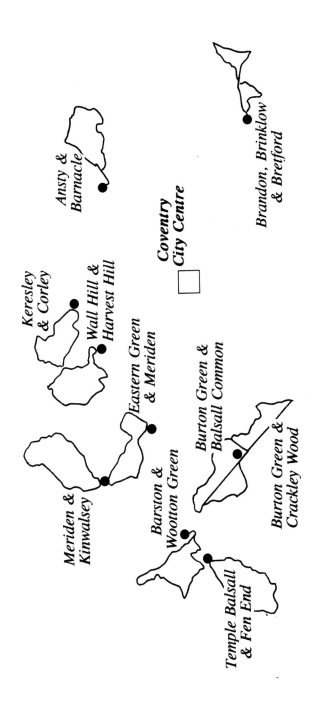

General Map

Ansty & Barnacle

Brandon, Brinklow & Bretford

Keresley & Corley

Wall Hill & Harvest Hill

Eastern Green & Meriden

Coventry City Centre

Meriden & Kinwalsey

Barston & Wootton Green

Burton Green & Balsall Common

Burton Green & Crackley Wood

Temple Balsall & Fen End

(7)

Meriden Shafts

The Country Code

* Enjoy the countryside and respect its life and work
* Guard against all risk of fire
* Fasten all gates
* Keep your dogs under close control
* Keep to public paths across farmland
* Use gates and stiles to cross fences, hedges and walls
* Leave livestock, crops and machinery alone
* Take your litter home
* Help to keep water clean
* Protect wildlife, plants and trees
* Take special care on country roads
* *Make no unnecessary noise*

Ansty & Barnacle

START?
Shopping centre at Ringwood Highway, Potters Green, Coventry.
This is about 1 mile west of M6 Junction 2 and the A46/Bypass
Map references: OS SP 375824, AZ 101 5H.

GETTING THERE?
Bus stop is at the shopping centre.

Park cars near the Jolly Colliers at the end of Woodway Lane,
which is the road crossing the end of Ringwood Highway. This
is on the walk so car travellers can start at paragraph (2).

Maps. OS Landranger 140 Leicester & Coventry, Pathfinder
935 SP 28/38, AZ 101 5H.

HOW FAR?
About 5.5 miles/9 kms.

REFRESHMENTS?
Apart from the Jolly Colliers at the start/end, we have the
Rose & Castle at Ansty and the Red Lion at Barnacle.

A CANAL & TWO VILLAGES
East of Coventry the landscape is mainly level, but this walk
rises surprisingly. After a stroll beside the canal you climb
gently past Ansty church to the small village of Barnacle and
return down a long slope.

The Oxford Canal links the Coventry Canal to the River
Thames. Started in 1769, it was an early part the system and
winds along the contours to avoid frequent changes of level
which require locks, cuttings and embankments. As engineer-
ing knowledge expanded and more investment was available
the later canals were bold and straight. On this section the
banks are garlanded with a bright mixture of wildflowers.

Ansty is a pleasant village with trees lining the main street and a cheerful jumble of new and old houses. Go and see the canalside potteries by the bridge. The main road is busy, but with the canal, it gives the place life without seeming to cause much disturbance. By contrast, Barnacle up on its hill seems very quiet and remote.

Ansty church is a grey sandstone Victorian job. A fragment of an older red stone church survives in the chancel. This is pocket gothic with a modest spire on an short octagonal tower. A niche over the west door drips with stone frillies and holds a diminutive knight looking sombre and elderly. Flanking him on stumpy, square, vaguely classical columns are two other miniature persons. One is wearing a cricket cap and holding a shield, so was probably next to bat in a West Indies match.

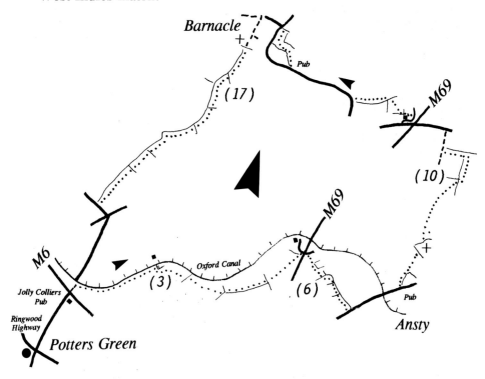

*(1) Face shopping centre &
go L to cross roads. Go L
400 yds to end of road &
pub.*

*(2) Cross M6 & just before
canal bridge, take steps
R. Follow towpath .4 mile
to 1st bridge & cross
stile R.*

*(3) Go L to end of trees.
Follow earth track
parallel with canal &
take gate. LEAVE TRACK,
go parallel with L hedge &
cross twin corner stiles.*

*(4) Go with fence on your
R & take gate. Go diag-
onally L to where fence
meets M69 & take gate to
track.*

*(5) Go R thro tunnel, then
cross stile R by shed. Go
to projecting hedge corner
then with hedge on your L
to its end . Keep same
line to BIGGEST tree &
cross fence beneath.*

*(6) Go with hedge on your
L (thro 2 hedge gaps) to
lane.*

*(7) Go L to Rose & Castle
& cross stile L.*

*(8) Go ahead to power
pole. Go R to church &
cross stile to churchyard.*◀

*(9) Go L to church car
park & cross stile. Pass
pond on your R, then go to
far R field corner & cross
stile.*

*(10)Go with hedge on your
L to corner. Go L thro
hedge gap, then with hedge
on your R to track. Go R
to road.*

*(11)Go L, cross M6 plus a
few paces & go R into
service road. Round L
bend & take small metal
gate L to garden.*

*(12) Follow path to far
hedge, bear L into corner
& cross stile. Cross field
diagonally & take stile.
Go L on field edge to lane*

*(13) Go ahead 500yds to
Village Hall R.*

*(14) Pass between chestnut
tree & Hall to join path.
Go with fence on your L to
end, then L to end of "L"
shaped field, gate & lane.*

*(15) Take lane opposite,
follow 200yds (via L
bend) to Park Farm sign.
Take path L.*

*(16) Follow to lane & go
ahead to chapel. Cross
stile ahead.* ➤

(11)

(17) Go with hedge on your R & thro 1st hedge gap to 2nd. DON'T GO THRO. Go with hedge on your R to next field corner & take gap R.

(18) Go .5 mile with hedge on your R (via 3 hedge) gaps) to allotments.

(19) Follow path past plots & cross stile, then path thro brambles etc to road.

(20) Go L to cross roads. Take Woodway Lane opposite 450yds. Cross canal & M6 back to start.

St Swithin's Church, Barston

(12)

Barston & Wootton Green

START?
Wootton Green Lane near the George in the Tree at Balsall
Common, which is on the A452 road north of Kenilworth.
Map references: OS SP 236778, AZ 128 1B.

GETTING THERE?
Bus Stop at junction of Kenilworth Road and Lavender Hall
Lane, Balsall Common.

Park Cars. Only use the pub car park with permission,
which might well be given if you intend to have a drink
later. For teetotallers there is limited parking in Wootton
Green Lane; go round the bend.

Maps. Landranger sheet 139 - Birmingham, Pathfinder SP
27/37 (955). AZ Birmingham etc.

HOW FAR?
The full walk is about 6.5 miles/11kms but we offer a short
version of 5.25 miles/9kms.

REFRESHMENTS?
The George in the Tree is at the start and the walk passes
the 13th century Saracen's Head and the Bull's Head at
Barston.

A VILLAGE, A RIVER, A BRIDGE & A LAKE.
The landscape round Barston and Balsall Common is almost
level, on the floor of the valley of the River Blythe. You
meet the river twice and some pools beside it, there is the
pretty village of Barston, an ancient packhorse bridge, and
for those who like this sort of thing, a railway.

As you walk the first field paths, you meet the Heart of England Way. If you followed this 100 mile Long Distance Footpath to the north you would pass through Meriden, Kingsbury Water Park, Lichfield and Cannock Chase. To the south are Berkswell, Henley in Arden, Alcester, Chipping Campden and Bourton on the Water.

The Saracen's Head is one of those comfortable old pubs. One wing was built in the 13th century. The sign shows the Saracen looking scornful and wearing a coal scuttle.

You can sense the agricultural past of the quiet village of Barston, but like many others, it is now a rural retreat for people working in Coventry and Solihull and a retirement home. St Swithin's church dates from the late 16th century but the basis of the present red brick church was built after a fire in 1721. The tower with its blue dialed clock and some other parts are obviously of this date, but the pointed windows of the nave look Victorian.

The River Blythe is 24 miles long and rises at Forshaw Heath to the west of Earlswood Lakes. The river supplies the lakes, passes around Solihull, and after a loop south at Barston, turns north past Hampton in Arden and Maxstoke to meet the River Tame at Hams Hall. It looks very fresh and clean and pretty on this walk, but because of several sewage works and the run off from roads and agriculture its water quality is only D on the National Rivers Authority's A to F scale.

The Blythe flows past Ryton End Pool, but the pool is quite modern and its water come not from the river but from the ground. These sand and gravel pits were abandoned some five years ago and with a little management, Warwickshire County Council have produced an attractive picnic area. Here you meet two contrasting bridges. The narrow, grey sandstone packhorse bridge crossing the River Blythe is medieval. The vast blue railway viaduct carries the main London - Birmingham line.

River Blythe

Bridges at Ryton End

(15)

(1) Enter Wootton Green Lane, round bend & pass last houses to take gate/stile L.

(2) Pass midfield oak on your L & cross midhedge stile. Bear R to projecting hedge corner, & go with hedge on your R to field corner.

(3) Go R thro hedge gap & with hedge on your L to cross corner stile. Head for far R corner & cross stile, then follow R hedge to cross next stile.

(4) Go ahead 50yds to stile R. DON'T CROSS. Go L parallel with L hedge & cross bottom stile under tree. Go ahead via bridge & cross stile, then with hedge on your R (via stiles) to road.

[Saracens Head pub is 200 yards left.]

(5) Go R 150 yds & take Barston Lane R. Follow 200 yds to R bend. Take wooded track L by gate.

(6) Follow 400yds & cross stile L. Follow L hedge into grove, cross stile L & cross bridge.

(7) Go ahead with fence on your L & take gate/stile L. Go with hedge on your R (via 2 stiles), then ahead to house & cross stile.

(8) Join track for 50yds to R bend & cross stile ahead. Bear R past projecting hedge corner & cross stile to churchyard. Pass church on your L to road. (Barston)

(9) Go R .3 mile, round L bend & take lane L. Follow for .5 mile to gate.

(10) Continue on track to end of L hedge, round R bend then L bend, & follow river to fork of tracks. Take R fork to T junction of sandy tracks.

****

ALTERNATIVES

For short route go next to para (10a). Full walk continues on para (11).

(10A) Go R, cross river. Follow lane 200yds to Marsh House Farm L & cross (?bust) stile R.

next para - (14) ➤
****

(11) Go L & follow R of 2 tracks. Join wide track with pool on your L to end of pool & round corner to barrier.

(12) Cross bridge R & follow path to lane. Go R, cross walkway & bridge & go on to L bend by rail bridge.

(13) Take track ahead to R bend & cross corner stile. Go with fence on your L for 2 stiles. Cross to

far R field corner & take stile. Go with hedge on your R (via stiles) to lane. Go R 12 paces to cross (?bust) stile L.

(14) Go with hedge on your R, pass sheds & cross stile. Cross field diagonally to stile, drive & lane.

(15) Take drive opposite & go straight to stables in OLD barn. Cross stile on its L, follow wall on your R & cross stile. With hedge/fence on your R, go 400yds (via stiles) to field corner with gate L.

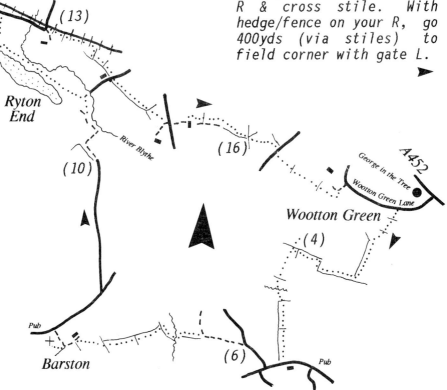

(13)

Ryton End

River Blythe

(10)

(16)

George in the Tree

A452

Wootton Green Lane

Wootton Green

(4)

Pub

Barston

(6)

Pub

(17)

(16) Take stile ahead & cross field diagonally to stile & lane. Go R 75yds to 1st gate L & cross stile.

(17) Go with hedge on your R & cross stile. Keep same line & take gate. Go with hedge on your L (via gateway) to end of wood, & take gate L.

(18) Go ahead to drive then R to bend of lane. Go R .5 mile to start.

"How did you sleep last night?"

Brandon, Brinklow & Bretford

START?
From the bus stop at the entrance to Coventry Stadium and opposite the Oakland Rose & Garden Centre. This is on the A428 Rugby road through Binley Woods. Map reference: OS SP 404773, not in the AZ.

GETTING THERE?
Bus Stop at the entrance to Coventry Stadium.

Park cars on the triangle of land by the stadium entrance.

Maps. Landranger 140 Leicester & Coventry, Pathfinder 956 SP 47/57. Not in the AZ.

HOW FAR?
About 5.5 miles/9 kms.

REFRESHMENTS?
At Brandon there is the Royal Oak, but it is half a mile off route and the link road is hazardous. The walk barely reaches the edge of Brinklow but there is a pub, again half a mile off. We redeem ourselves at Bretford with the Queens Head.

SANDY TRACKS & SKY
These long sandy tracks through miles of flat fields have a silent and mysterious charm. Where do they go and why are they here? The fringe of woodland gives shelter and food to wildlife which would otherwise have vanished from this heavily farmed landscape.

Brinklow has a fine little church and an Iron Age Fort later used by the Romans. It is on the Fosse Way from Exeter to Lincoln. So is Bretford, which also has a tired old bridge over the River Avon.

(1) From stadium entrance pass garden centre on your R & go 350yds. By 2nd stadium entrance take track L.

(2) Go 300yds to end of iron fence L & take hedge gap R into field.

(3) Go with hedge on your R to its corner. LOOK AHEAD at 1st & 2nd tree clumps. Pass both close on your R, then bear a little L to sign boards at road bend.

(4) Take track L .75 mile (via small gate & L bend) to T junction.

(5) Go R 100yds to gates. Fork L for .85 mile to start of lane.

(6) Follow .3 mile to houses L by sharp L bend with track R.

(7) Follow track (past gateway L) .65 mile to fence posts R by cross ways.

(8) Take track AHEAD (not curving L) .3 mile to road at Bretford.

(9) Go R, pass driveway & take track R. Follow .8 mile (at fork go either way) to 2 gates & outward track.

(10) Go ahead .8 mile (past track L & houses) to start.

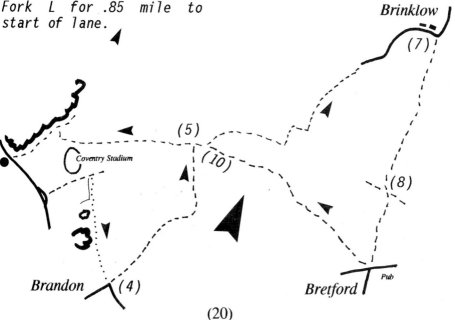

Brinklow

(7)

(5)

Coventry Stadium

(10)

(8)

Brandon   (4)

Bretford   Pub

(20)

Burton Green
& Balsall Common

START?
From the railway bridge by the junction of Cromwell Lane and Hodgett's Lane, Burton Green, Coventry. This is just over a mile south of Tile Hill railway station. Map references: OS SP 269759, AZ 129 4H.

GETTING THERE?
Bus stop is at the junction above.

Train. Tile Hill station is about a mile north on Cromwell Lane. You could also start (or bottle out) about half way round this walk at Berkswell station. To start there begin at paragraphs (14) or (14a).

Park cars in Hodgett's Lane opposite or beyond the last houses. Do not use the Village Hall car park which is likely to be in use on most days.

Maps. Landrangers 140 Leicester & Coventry with a fragment of the walk on 139 Birmingham, Pathfinder 955 SP 27/37, AZ Birmingham etc.

HOW FAR?
There is an alternative to the main walk which is a bit shorter. Main walk 6 miles/9.5 kms, alternative 5 miles/8.5 kms.

REFRESHMENTS?
On Cromwell Lane and about half a mile from the start is The Peeping Tom. At Berkswell is The Railway.

FIELDS & RAILWAYS
This landscape easy and level but there are many unexpected little dips and rises, a good deal of grassland and many trees Notice the two distinct types of field. Some are

large, square and open and tend to be under arable crops. Others are small and narrow with crooked hedges beside a stream or railway. These are usually pasture.

You see a lot of the Birmingham - London main railway line. This was one of the great pioneer lines completed by George and Robert Stephenson in 1837 and became part of the London & North Western Railway, which in 1923 was the largest part of the London, Midland & Scottish Railway (LMS). Curious then to find a fine picture at The Railway pub by Berkswell station of a Great Western Railway Castle class locomotive. No doubt a few did thunder past, but a crimson Royal Scot would have been more appropriate. Even odder are the madly green coaches in no livery ever seen on a British railway.

The alternative walk follows a disused railway. This was a late built spur connecting the main line to the Coventry - Kenilworth - Leamington line.

(1) From end of Hodgett's Lane face Cromwell Lane & go L. Follow road .6 mile, pass pub plus 150 yds, & by No. 172 take track L.

(2) Follow to end & cross stile. Go ahead passing power pole on your L, then midfield tree, & cross hedge corner stile.

(3) Head for bottom R field corner (if path blocked follow R edge) & cross stile. Bear L to fieldside mound, then with hedge on your R (via stile & gate) to lane.

(5) Go L 100yds to drive L & cross stile opposite. Head 50yds L of white house & cross stile to lane.

(6) Go R & cross railway, plus 25yds to 1st house. Take track L to end gate & cross stile.

(7) Go with hedge on your R 400yds (via stiles) to track, & follow it to lane

(8) Go L 50yds & enter drive R to Moat Farm House. Go 100yds, round L bend, pass gate L & cross stile L.

(9) Go ahead & cross stile, then with hedge on your R to stile & drive. Go R to R bend. Bear L across field to BIGGEST oak in opposite hedge.

(10) Go with hedge on your R, round bottom field corner & cross plank bridge. Cross stile L. Go to far field end stile & lane.

(11) Go L 20yds & cross stile R. Go with stream on your L & cross bridge, then ahead (via gate/stile) to cross railway & stile.

(12) Go L by railway & cross 2 stiles, then to far R field corner & take hedge gap to track. Go L to road.

(13) Go L & cross road to sunken road. At station car park gate, take stile by gate R.

(14) Follow narrow fields thro 2 gate/stiles. Go with hedge on your R 80yds to midhedge gate R.

(10)

Railway Station

Pub

Balsall Common

(15)

(8)

(17)

(3)

Pub

disused railway

water tower

Hodgetts Lane

Cromwell Lane

(22)

Beanit Farm

Burton Green

◄ main walk
continues para (15)

****
ALTERNATIVE

You can follow a disused
railway back to the start.

(14a) Turn L, cross field
to opposite hedge & take
stile. Follow fenced path
(via stile) to trackbed.

(14b) Follow 1.7 miles
under 1st road bridge
(half way) to 2nd.

(14c) Go on 200yds to meet
path from L. Follow it
back to last bridge &
start.
****

(15) Take midhedge gate R
& go L. Pass projecting
hedge corner, cross twin
stiles & on to cross next
stile.

(16) Bear R across field &
take midhedge gate/stile.
Go with hedge on your L to
cross stile & bridge. Keep
same line to corner with
stiles ahead & L. ◄

(17) Cross stile L, follow
◄ R hedge 50yds & cross
stile by gate R. Follow
hedged track to lane. Go R
to road.

(18) Go L a few paces &
cross to take gate on L
of house. Go ahead to
hedge corner, then on to
take gate ahead. Bear L
to sheds & follow track to
road.

(19) Go L .4 mile, pass
Hill Farm R plus 100yds &
take drive L to Beanit
Farm.

(20) Follow 30yds to phone
pole R & just beyond cross
fence/stile R. Cross end
of rough field & take
stile & bridge L. Go
ahead past shed corner &
keep same line to pond.
Bear R to track.

(21) Go L 300yds to end of
track by ponds & cross
double stile. Go ahead &
cross corner stile.

(22) Cross field diagon-
ally between pylon & tree
& take corner stile to
railway.

(23) Cross & follow stone
path R thro trees to lane.
Go R to start. ●

Burton Green
& Crackley Wood

START?
From the railway bridge by the junction of Cromwell Lane and Hodgett's Lane, Burton Green, Coventry. This is just over a mile south of Tile Hill railway station. Map references: OS SP 269759, AZ 129 4H.

GETTING THERE?
Bus stop is at the junction above.

Train. Tile Hill station is about a mile north on Cromwell Lane.

Park cars in Hodgett's Lane opposite or beyond the last houses. Do not use the Village Hall car park which is likely to be in use on most days.

Maps Landrangers 140 Leicester & Coventry with a fragment of the walk on 139 Birmingham, Pathfinder 955 SP 27/37, AZ Birmingham etc.

HOW FAR?
About 5.5 miles/8.6 kms.

REFRESHMENTS?
The Peeping Tom is on Cromwell Lane at the end of the walk.

A RAILWAY & A WOOD
This old railway was a link between the main Birmingham Coventry - London line at Berkswell station and the Coventry - Leamington Spa line at Kenilworth. It was closed by the dreaded Dr Beeching and the track lifted, but old country railways are often of little use apart from a few stations and areas like shunting yards. This one was pur-ased by Warwickshire County Council in 1973 to form a walking and cycling track, or

"greenway". Not much progress has been made but in the meantime, the excellent and efficient Kenilworth Footpaths Society have been allowed to make it walkable, so you can use it.

Old railways all over Britain are being converted to this type of use but not so many in this part of the Midlands. We have a line from west of Dudley to Tettenhall, Wolverhampton and the line from Stratford upon Avon to Long Marston.

At the far end of this walk the railway line passes through Crackley Wood which is owned by the County Council and managed by Warwickshire Wildlife Trust. You could leave the footpath and wander about. Magnificent sweet chestnuts dominate the south side which is open and airy, to the north are craggy and mishapen oaks, much birch and a dense understory of bracken, hazel and brambles. Growing through it all is holly. There are odd patches of Scots pine, sycamore and ash.

(1) On Hodgett's Lane end of railway bridge, take path between garden fence & end bridge pillar. Follow path down to trackbed.

(2) Go ahead 2 miles (crossing over 2 lanes & going thro wood) to blue brick arched bridge.

(3) Take steps up R to stile & track. Go L to its end & take small gate. Go with hedge on your L & take small corner gate.

(4) Follow fenced path .4 mile to lane.

(5) Continue on fenced path opposite about same distance & take small gate to track.

(6) Go ahead a few paces & cross stile R (not small gate). Cross field corner to 50yds L of wood & take stile. KEEP SAME LINE & (when in view) go up to BIG gatepost & stile.

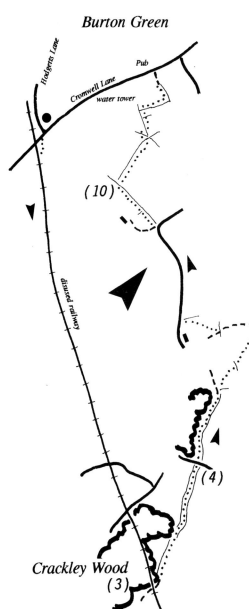

(7) DO NOT CROSS. Take rough track L to next hedge & cross corner stile. Cross field diagonally to stile & lane.

(8) Go R .4 mile to sharp R bend & farm gate L.

(9) Cross stile on R of gate. Go with hedge/fence on your R (via 2 stiles) & take midfence gate/stile R

(10) Go with hedge on your L & cross corner stile L, then next corner stile. Go L to field corner & cross stile, then cross next stile to sports field.

(11) Go R to far side fence. DON'T CROSS STILES. Go L to gateway & cross stile on its R.

(12) Follow hedged path to road. (Cromwell Lane) Go L to start.

Eastern Green & Meriden

START?
Poachers Retreat pub at junction of Upper Eastern Green Lane,
Hockley Lane and Pickford Green Lane, Upper Eastern Green.
This is .5 mile north of the Massey Ferguson works. Map
references: OS SP 274803, AZ 114 3A and 113 3H.

GETTING THERE?
Bus Stop is opposite the Poachers Retreat.

Park Cars. Considerate kerbside parking can be found nearby.
Only use the pub car park with permission.

Maps Landrangers 139 Leicester & Coventry and 140 Birmingham, Pathfinder 935 SP 28/38, AZ Birmingham etc.

HOW FAR?
About 5miles/8kms.

REFRESHMENTS?
There is the Poacher's Retreat at the start and the Queen's
Head, Meriden half way round. [Take path through Meriden
churchyard and down fields to road. Cross and take steps to
pub.]

TWO CHURCHES IN A QUIET LANDSCAPE
On this side of Coventry the ground slopes gently upwards to
a broad, low ridge on which Meriden church stands. This is
not dramatic landscape, but a pleasantly undulating pattern
of hedges, fields and woods which makes for an easy and
relaxing walk.

At the start you pass St Andrew's church, red brick with blue
bands and stone dressing. That steep little spire on its octagonal tower is far from the traditional English parish church
but this romantic, high Victorian style has become just

as much a part of the scene. The church is guarded by two gigantic and very attractive wellingtonia trees from North America.

In complete contrast, St Lawrence's church on its hill above Meriden was founded in the 11th century and some Norman parts remain. Most of the present building was completed in the 16th century but there are Victorian extensions and additions. It sits amongst the gravestones and the native yew trees.

Meriden Church

(29)

(1) From cross roads follow Church Lane past church & take farm gate. Go thro via 2 gates & take gateway to field with pylon.

(2) Go L to field corner & cross stile (NOT GATE). Go with hedge on your L & cross stile to track. Follow it to lane.

(3) Go R .5 mile passing Woodlands, Greenways Farm & Back Lane Farm to next house, "The Byre", & take track R.

(4) Pass gate R & cross stile. Go ahead to fence corner & cross stile. Bear L to bottom L field corner gate & cross stile.

(5) Go with hedge on your R & cross stile, then pass 2 gates R & cross stile. Go with hedge on your R & cross field bottom stile.

(6) Go up with hedge on your R, pass top power pole, round field corner & take gate to lane.◢

(7) Go R & round church. Pass white house L to next L bend by "Fentham".

(8) Take track R & cross stile. Bear R parallel with R hedge to field corner, & take gate.

(9) Follow fenced track to end & take gate. Go on past 1st gate L to 2nd & cross stile.

(10) NOTE wood on L of field. Head for its far end & cross stile in hedge corner (NOT INTO WOOD).

(11) Go R with hedge on your R (via 2 stiles) to field corner with power pole.

(12) Take stone track L via gates (becomes tarmac) to lane.

(13) Go R 250yds to junction, then L 80yds & take steps R. ►

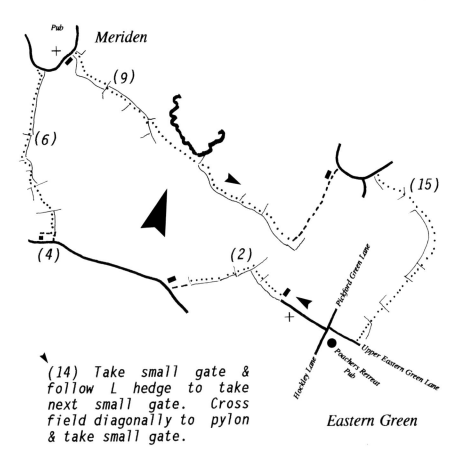

Meriden

(9)

(6)

(15)

(4)

(2)

Pickford Green Lane

Hockley Lane

Poachers Retreat Pub

Upper Eastern Green Lane

Eastern Green

(14) Take small gate & follow L hedge to take next small gate. Cross field diagonally to pylon & take small gate.

(15) Go ahead to L of small pylon, then with hedge on your R (via R bend & small gates) to end of track with bridge L.

(16) Cross, go to top R field corner & take gateway. Keep same line & take small gate.

(17) Go with hedge on your L & take small gate to road. Go L to start. ●

(31)

Keresley & Corley

START?
The junction of Bennetts Road South and Watery Lane, Keresley
by the bus stop and Hare & Hounds pub. The Coventry Colliery
is just to the north. Map references; OS SP 319838, AZ 3H99.

GETTING THERE?
Bus Stop is by the Hare & Hounds.

Parking is difficult and limited. In quiet periods there is
kerb space in Fivefield Lane. Only use the Hare & Hounds car
park with permission.

Maps. Landranger 139 Leicester & Coventry, Pathfinder 935
SP 28/38. AZ Birmingham etc.

HOW FAR?
About 5 mile/8kms.

REFRESHMENTS?
The Hare & Hounds at the start is the only pub.

SMALL HILLS, SOME WOODS & A ROCK
The true shape of this landscape of small hills is disguised
by woods, hedges, farms and houses, but it is part of a much
bigger piece of Midlands geography. From the Tamworth area
on the edge of the Trent Valley a chain of hills runs south,
swings west of Coventry and peters out into the valley of the
Avon. The high points are the formidable hills near Nuneaton.

Near the start of the walk is an attractive little wood with
oak, ash, birch, holly and the usual understorey of brambles
and bracken. Look out for the rowan trees in the top corner,
in autumn they are dressed with red berries. From the wood

Keresley's colossal coal plant has vanished; you are high on a country hill with a view of the city far below.

You approach Corley rocks from their least impressive side and realise only gradually how high and steep is this outcrop of red sandstone. You can leave the lane at paragraph (7) to wander over it. Although once an Iron Age hill fort, the fortifications are hard to see in the hawthorn, hazel and oak. In any case, the cunning Britons have disguised it as a litter bin to fool the Romans.

Corley's church is compact and unpretentious with a squat little bellcote. Much of it seems to be Victorian restoration or extension, but go and see the south side. There are round headed windows and a door which look Norman.

The walk ends with a surprise. The coal works has come in view but your path suddenly drops so that it disappears and you follow the shallow, green valley of the Hall Brook.

Corley Rocks

(33)

(1) From Hare & Hounds go to T junction. Go R & take 1st L (Fivefield Lane) for 300yds to L bend.

(2) Take track ahead, pass garage on your R & cross stile. Pass midfield oak on your R, then keep same line to cross midhedge stile

(3) Head for top L field corner & cross stile. Go R by wood to cross top field corner stile.

(4) Go down to cross bottom R field corner stile. (If path obstructed follow R field edge.)

(5) Go R & cross stile onto FENCED path. Cross next stile, then with hedge on your L to cross corner stile.

(6) Go with hedge on your R to power pole, plus 50yds to hedge gap R. Go R with HEDGE ON YOUR R & join hollow track thro rock to gateway & lane.

(7) Go L to T junction. Go R 100yds & take small gate L.

(8) Go with fence on your R & cross (?bust) stile. Go parallel with L hedge & cross stile R of thatched cottage to road. (Corley)

(9) Take lane opposite .3 mile towards mast & cross stile R just before house.

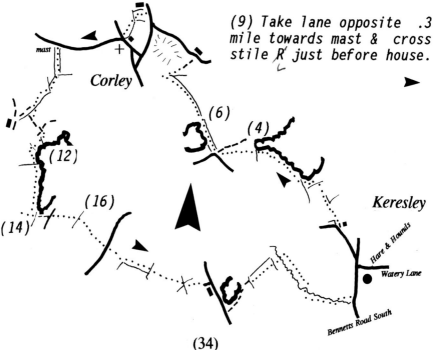

(10) Follow fenced path & cross stile. Go with hedge on your R & cross stile, then with fence on your L towards track to cross stile L.

(11) Cross next stile to track & go down to L bend. Take gateway ahead. Go diagonally R & cross stile where fence meets wood.

(12) Go with wood on your L (via stile) to corner, plus a few yards to field corner. Cross 2 stiles L.

(13) Follow edge of wood 350yds & cross stile L.

(14) Go up past kennels to stile & lane. Take drive opposite & go straight thro sheds to track bend. Cross stile opposite.

(15) LOOK AHEAD to far field edge. From R note single trees then long line. Head for middle of LINE & cross valley stile.

(16) Bear a little R & rise upfield. LOOK AHEAD & WHEN IN VIEW note line of single trees from L, then bushes. Head for bushes & cross stile to lane.

(17) Go L a few paces & cross stile. Go with hedge on your L & cross corner stile, then with hedge on your R to take gateway.

(18) Cross field diagonally L & take corner stile to paddock. (If field obstructed follow L edge).

(19) Cross to near side of shed & take small gate. Go L & take gate to drive & B4098.

(20) Cross, go R 300yds to wood corner & take track L. Follow wood edge to corner & cross stile ahead. Go down field edge & cross off-corner stile. Cross small field, then next stile & brook.

(21) Go R with brook on your R to field corner & cross bridge R. Go with hedge on your L & cross stile.

(22) Go on 150yds past gate L, take hedge gap L & cross stile. Go with hedge on your R road. Go L to start. ●

Woods of different character.

*Oak, ash, birch, holly and
◄ rowan with brambles and
bracken near Keresley.*

*Sunlight filters onto open
ground under the alders by
the River Blythe.*
▼

NJF.

(36)

Meriden & Kinwalsey

START?
From the Queen's Head pub on the B4102, which is the road through Meriden from the A45. The pub is in a small loop off the main road half a mile east of the village and opposite the church. Map reference: OS SP 252820, AZ 97 5E.

GETTING THERE?
Bus Stop. About 250 yards on the village side of the Queen's Head. Services 192Y, 194Y, 900. *[From bus stop walk to foot of hill and take old road left to the pub.]*

Park Cars. Roadside parking in the loop; be very considerate. Only use the pub car park with permission.

Maps. Landranger 139 Birmingham, Pathfinder 935 SP28/38.

HOW FAR?
About 5.5 miles/9 kms.

REFRESHMENTS?
Nothing on the walk, but at the start we have the Queen's Head and in Meriden, the Bull's Head and some restaurants.

HIGH POINTS, WOODS & THE MIDDLE OF ENGLAND
This walk rises to a modest high point and the return falls gently down the shoulder of a hill. From several places in the area there are views of central Birmingham.

Oak tree waymarks on the first section of the walk tell you that this is the Heart of England Way which stretches 100 miles from near Stafford to the Cotswolds. It started as an idea from some rambling clubs and volunteers worked for ten years, mending stiles and bridges, clearing undergrowth and talking to farmers, before the County and District Councils took an interest. It is still maintained by members of the HoEW Association. For information contact WALKWAYS.

You meet several woods but this traditionally "leafy" county has only some 3% tree cover compared with twice as much in other Midland counties. The first wood is Meriden Shafts, named because of past mining in shallow pits, and you will meet Close, Church and Birchley Hayes Woods. All have probably been woodland for many centuries, possibly since the last Ice Age, but except for the last wood they are now under conifers and of little wildlife interest.

Meriden claims to be at the centre of England and marks the spot with a 14th century market cross. Norman portions of the church remain but the present building was completed in the 16th century. Now it sits amongst a scatter of old gravestones, the archetypal English parish church. The village has a pond, a post office, a couple of shops and restaurants and the Bull's Head. It has long been popular with cyclists who erected a memorial on the green to those who had died in the two world wars.

(1) Face Queens Head & take lane on its R (not slip road). Follow .75 mile past L fork, under A45, past L fork & caravan park.

(2) After next bungalow L cross stile L. Follow R hedge & cross stile.

(3) Go down midfield & thro gappy hedge. Bear L to cross corner plank bridge.◀

(4) Cross stile & follow wood path up to stile & track. Go L 50 yds & cross stile R.

(5) Follow R hedges (via 3 fields) to lane.

(6) Go L 300yds to sharp L bend, power pole & "Harvest Hill Lane" sign. (? bust, lost or rotted).

(7) Cross stile R. Go ahead midfield & cross stile & bridge to wood edge track. ▶

(38)

(8) Go L past wood. Follow L hedge round field end & cross stile to lane.

(9) Go L to end of farm wall & take gate R. Bear L past corner of barn to field corner & cross stile. Go with hedge on your L, pass ponds & take gate.

(10) Go with hedge on your R to field corner & cross stile. Go parallel with L hedge to R of grey corner house, & cross stile to lane.

(11) Go L .4 mile & pass mast L to corner of wood R

(12) Cross stile R & follow path with wood on your R till it enters wood.

(13) Go ahead & cross 2 paths to fork. Go R to wood edge & cross stile.

(14) NOTE dutch barn L of farm buildings and head for R end. Leave field & cross end of barn to track

(15) Go R & pass farm gate on your R, then with hedge on your R to take gateway. Go with HEDGE ON YOUR L & take next gate L.

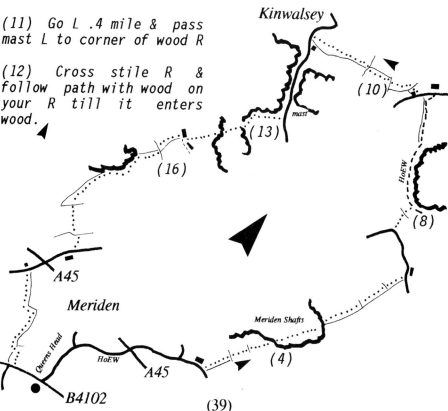

Kinwalsey

mast

(10)

(13)

(16)

HoEW

(8)

A45

Meriden

Meriden Shafts

HoEW

A45

(4)

Queens Head

B4102

(39)

(16) Go with HEDGE ON YOUR R, then beside wood to its corner & cross stile. Go R with wood, then hedge on your R (via 2 stiles), & cross off-corner stile L.

(17) IF path not visible, go ahead bearing slightly left, & (when in view) head 10yds from L end of bushes to enter gap. Go thro thicket & cross stile. Head for R side of white house & cross stile to B4102.

(18) Cross, go R 350yds to phone pole L & enter track L.

(19) Go only 8 paces & turn R thro hedge gap to field. Follow deep ditch L, zig L & zag R, then with hedge on your L to field corner by shed.

(20) Go R to projecting hedge corner & follow L fence 18 paces to cross stile L. Bear R & cross stile to road. Go L back to start.

Chapel of the Knight's Templar

Temple Balsall & Fen End

START?
From the Saracen's Head pub on the B4101 Balsall Common -
Knowle road at the junction with Magpie Lane. This spot is
about 1 mile west of Balsall Common. Map references: OS
SP 224771, AZ 128 2A.

GETTING THERE?
Buses. A few go to the Saracen's Head, but there is a better
service to the junction of Balsall Street and Station Road.

Park Cars. Parking is limited by there is a service road
which one car may use considerately. Only use the pub car
park with permission, though offering to eat or drink at
the Saracen's Head after your walk is no great burden.

Maps. Landranger sheet 139 Birmingham, Pathfinder 955
SP 27/37, AZ Birmingham etc.

HOW FAR?
About 5.5 miles/9 kms.

REFRESHMENTS?
Apart from the Saracen's Head, teas can be had at the Alms
Houses in Temple Balsall on summer weekends.

FIELDS, STREAMS & CRUSADERS
This walk first crosses a big dome of land with broad fields,
then falls gently into the valley of the River Blythe. A more
intimate landscape follows, with small fields, close hedges
and tiny lanes. You cross six little streams, all tributaries
of the Blythe. This is one of four walks in the book which
meets the Heart of England Way. See *Eastern Green &
Meriden* and *Meriden & Kinwalsey* for details.

The Saracen whose head is on the pub sign does not look the sort of chap who would buy you a pint, but his pub is more friendly. The oldest part is 13th century. The name suggests a connection with the crusades which is confirmed by the Hall and Chapel of the Knights Templars at Temple Balsall.

As you leave the little settlement around the pub you pass two fine houses. Magpie Farm is a dazzling example of a timbered Warwickshire farmhouse, and nearby is Balsall Farm, red brick with sandstone quoins.

Temple Balsall is secluded and not quite of this world. The name derives from the Knights Templars, soldier monks who held the land in the 12th and 13th centuries. The alms houses and a school for poor boys were founded in the late 17th century by Lady Katherine Leveson. They are built of warm red brick in that most dignified yet domestic of styles and ranged around a court. The present church is largely Victorian by Sir Gilbert Scot; crocketts on every spire and ridge. Go and see the organ, like a huge dark, wedding cake, and the splendid tiled floor of the choir. The Old Hall is what remains of the medieval foundation. It has a brick dressing but much of the timber is original.

(1) Take Magpie Lane by pub 75yds (past house) to power pole. Cross stile & go to bottom L field corner stile & lane.

(2) Go L past farm & cross stile R. Go ahead round field edge & projecting fence corner to open field.

(3) Head for gap L of centre in bottom hedge & cross BRIDGE. Go ahead

to cross midhedge stile. Follow L hedge (via stile) & cross top stile.

(4) Go with hedge on your R .4 mile to lane.

(5) Go R, round R bend, pass Temple House & take path L (Alms Houses etc).

(6) Follow past church & cross brook to gates ahead & each side. Take kissing gate L. Go with hedge on your L to track.

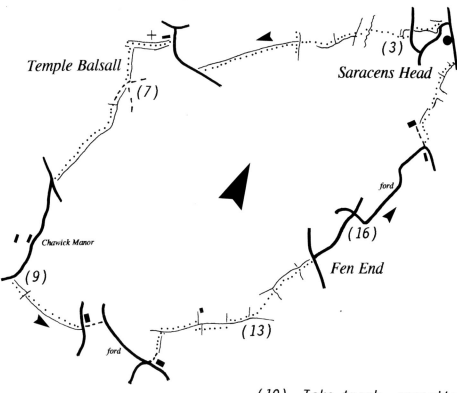

Temple Balsall

(7)

(3)

Saracens Head

ford

(16)

Chawick Manor

Fen End

(9)

(13)

ford

(7) Go R on track to gate & field, then with hedge on your L .5 mile to lane.

(8) Go R a few paces to junction, then L (Chadwick Lane). Follow .4 mile (past Court, Grange & big conifers R plus 100yds) to cross stile L.

(9) Go with hedge on your L & cross stile. Keep same line past projecting hedge corner & (via gate) to stile & lane.

(10) Take track opposite to lane. Go R .3 mile up to farm L.

(11) Take track L & pass farm on your R (via gate & stile), then with hedge on your R to cross corner stile & bridge.

(12) Go R by hedge & cross corner stile. Go with hedge on your L 300yds (via high stile) to hedge kink, & cross stile L.

(13) Go down with hedge on your R & cross hidden corner stile. Cross bridge. Head for top L field corner tree & cross stile.

(14) Go to top L field corner & cross stile, then with hedge on your L (round tennis courts) to stile & lane.

(15) Go R a few paces & take lane L (Longbrook) 400yds to junction.

(16) Go R (Fernhill Lane) .4 mile(under power lines & up hill) to R bend with farm R.

(17) Enter gates L & take iron gate R. Go with hedge on your L past farm to gateway L.

(18) Step thro & go with hedge on your R to its corner. Keep same line past projecting hedge corner & cross corner stile.

(19) Go ahead to R field corner, cross stile & follow fenced path to B4101.

Wall Hill & Harvest Hill

START?
The bus stop with turning loop at Brownshill Green by the junction of Browns Lane and Hawkes Mill Lane. This is about .5 mile north-east of the Jaguar works. Map references: OS SP 304827, AZ 99 4E.

GETTING THERE?
Bus Stop as above.

Park Cars. Limited parking in Hawkes Mill Lane. The White Lion pub at the junction of Hawkes Mill Lane and Wall Hill Lane has a car park, but only use it with permission.

Maps Landranger 140 - Leicester & Coventry, Pathfinder SP 28/38. AZ Birmingham etc

HOW FAR?
About 5.5 mile/8.75 kms.

REFRESHMENTS
The White Lion at the start is the only pub.

ROLLING FIELDS AND SMALL HILLS
This is a landscape of rolling green fields and small hills, with woodland, hedges and many small ponds. There are pleasant open views, no villages and rather few houses and farms. It is not obvious, but you walk first up the small hills forming the west side of the valley of the tiny River Shebourne and later down the east side. You only meet the river at the end as it nears the urban area where it is joined by the Pickford Brook. The Sherbourne flows, or trickles, right through the city centre to join the River Sowe at the Lunt Roman fort.

(1) From T junction cross to 40mph sign opposite Browns Lane. Take hedged path, then follow field edge to lane.

(2) Go L 100yds to City boundary post & take small gate L. Go ahead to corner of L hedge by house. Bear L to pass projecting fence corner on your R & take small gates. Go ahead to pylon & track.

(3) Go L 50yds to back of bungalow. Take fenced path R & take small gate. Go ahead to gate & track.

(4) Take small gate opposite & pass house on your R. Follow track to fork by houses.

(5) Go R & take L of 2 gates. Pass house & take small gate. Go with hedge on your R (via 2 gates) to lane.

(6) Go L 80yds to traffic sign & cross stile R. Bear L across field corner to cross stile & bridge. Go R along hedge to stile & lane. ◢

(7) Cross stile opposite. Bear L across field corner & cross stile L of ash tree. Go ahead, pass tree clump close on your L & cross stile.

(8) Bear L with power lines & cross stile. Go with hedge on your L & round top field corner to cross twin stiles.

(9) Go ahead parallel with L hedge. Pass power pole close on your L to pylon, & cross corner stile to lane.

(10) CARE - TRAFFIC. Go R .3 mile & pass lane R. Go on 50yds to just past house & take small gate L.

(11) Go ahead to L of shed & take small gate, then with hedge on your R & take small gate. Go ahead to house & take small gate to track.

(12) Go R & cross stile, Go with hedge on your R .25 mile (via small gates & L curve) to small gate by brick shed.

(13) Go ahead passing pond on your L & take small gate to lane. Go ahead up to L bend by house. ▶

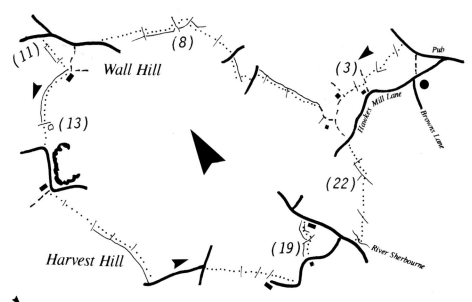

(14) Take track R 70yds & take small gate L. Follow L hedge to its corner, then keep same line ahead & take midfence gate.

(15) Go ahead & take mid fence gate. Go with hedge on your R (via gates & R bend) to cross timber walkway. Go ahead between houses to lane.

(16) Go L .25 mile to T junction & cross stile opposite.

(17) Go ahead between midfield trees & take gate. Bear L & cross mid fence stile, then ahead & cross stile. Go with hedge on your R & cross field corner stile to track.

(18) Go L 200yds to house & cross stile by gate L.

(19) Bear R to far power pole & cross concrete bridge. Follow path (becomes track) round R bend & take gate. Go ahead (via gate) by road.

(20) Go R 400yds yds & cross stile L.

(21) Cross next stile & bridge. Cross field diagonally & take R of 2 gates. Keep same line & cross top corner stile.

(22) Go L to hedge corner & cross stile. Go ahead towards house & cross stile to lane.

(23) Go R .4 mile to start.

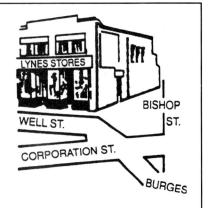